Screenplay: The Ultimate Step by Step Tutorial for Screenwriting Made Easy

by Neo Monefa

Table of Contents

14. THANK YOU FOR READING !

1. Introduction

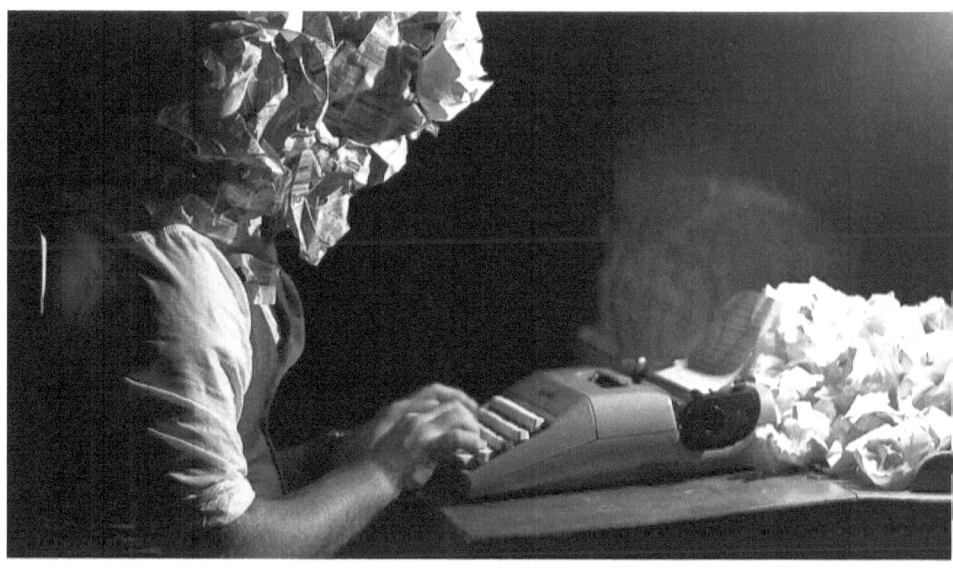

Hollywood is experiencing a big boom with aspiring screenwriters. Competition in Hollywood is very tough, but armed with the right knowledge you can overcome any obstacle and conquer the movie industry. My job here

is to help you, by creating this book filled with strategies, tricks of the trade, and useful methods that will help you create a successful screenplay.

You have already taken the first step forward: conceiving an idea for a movie. Now, by reading this book, you've shown that you're ready to move forward and take the necessary steps to be successful in Hollywood. When you're done reading this, you'll be armed with the tools that you'll need and give the industry a run for their money!

Hollywood is always hungry for new ideas, and if you've got the right ones up your sleeve, you could be apart of movie magic in just a few years. The motion picture industry is one of the most lucrative and challenging in the world, and here you have an opportunity to create movies that will leave a lasting impression on generations to come. You have the power to create unforgettable lines that people will repeat, and talk about for hours. You have a chance to change lives and bring people even temporary relief from the madness that is their own reality. In a few years from now, people could be paying up to $50 per movie ticket, based on an study by Entertainment Weekly's recent articles. People are willing to pay their hard earned money for two hours or so of entertainment, comic relief, and drama that you have the power to make materialize, from inception of idea to the big screen.

Just like with other things in life, taking that big leap into screenwriting requires careful, methodical planning. This is why it's not uncommon to hear of writers who take breaks lasting many months or more, in a quiet place just to get the writing done. Go where you need to go, do what you to do which will allow you to focus on the task at hand. But don't worry, because I'm here to give you the essential tools you'll need to write your screenplay, each step tried and tested by all the successful screenwriters in
Hollywood. I can't emphasize the importance of a well written screenplay; it is the form and foundation of which your future in the movie industry will rely on.

Take Alfred Hitchcock, for example. He is a legend in the movie industry, and he spent most of his time reading and researching scripts. This is because he understands the importance of the script, and imagines that he's only worked in one genre in the industry his whole life. If you are interested in spanning multiple genres, then there is much more work you have to do. But be patient, you will get there! in time.

A good script will help you create the outline, and provide a structure to the ideas you've got in mind.

Before you start moving forward, here are some key points:

1. Work on your outline first.

The outline is also known as a "beat sheet" in the industry, which has been known to be helpful before writers begin the tedious work of launching into their script. Also, having an outline beforehand will prevent you from working in circles. I personally find it easier to work on characters first, followed by my outline, then the script. This is when I see the story really starting to materialize and come to life.

2. Most writers, when starting out, tend to make the mistake of changing essential concepts in the first draft before even finishing it.

This is because they end up realizing that the original story needs major tweaking, when in fact you haven't seen it to fruition. But I need to tell you now, before you change anything, finish your fist draft. Work on one idea to the end, before you decide to change it. By constantly procrastinating and avoiding the ending by changing things several times over, you aren't doing anything productive but simply keeping up the habit of avoiding finishing anything. Don't be so hard on yourself; we've all written terrible first drafts. However, remember that the only way to get to an excellently written tenth draft is by first working on your initial draft.

3. Read as many screenplays as possible, this will serve as your well of inspiration. Expose yourself to all the great minds of the film industry, from the classics to the modern geniuses. There's no excuse for not being able to find screenplays as the Internet is a treasure chest of screenplays in script format to guide you along the way. Study scripts in the genre you'd like to write for.

4. Get some people together who love to write.

Some screenwriters find that having a support group is one of the most helpful things you can do to move forward in your career. I recommend meeting at least once a week, to help provide constructive criticism on each other's scripts. It can be challenging to find readers, so a group of writers is the next best thing. They can see things in your script that you may not have realized in the beginning, and their feedback can provide great insight on your story. This way you'll know if your joke is really effective, when other writers in the group get it. The group ideally should be supportive at its core; this isn't meant to be a group where you can tear down each other's work and throw all the negative comments around. Find the positives in the work, and be honest about what you think of a story.

5. Screenwriting is truly laborious.

If you want to succeed in this industry, accept this fact for all that it can be. Some people just never stop writing altogether.

6. Just keep going.

Good, honest, hard work will eventually lead you to the right opportunities that you need to kick start your career in Hollywood. Don't judge others that you meet along the way, for their choices or methods of doing things. We're all in this together, and meeting the same kinds of struggles.

The process of writing your first screenplay, or any screenplay for that matter is a long term commitment. It's a marathon, more than it is a sprint. Don't be intimidated by others in the industry that can whip out the next blockbuster in just a few weeks. Everyone has their own pace, and their own processes to consider. Most of all just enjoy what you do and have fun doing it!

2. What's a Logline?

The logline is the the very heart and essence of the entire screenplay. This should be one of the most carefully thought out aspects of creating a compelling movie because if your log line is vague the rest of the elements will also be vague. The logline is usually written after you are done producing your script. This is because the logline represents a condensed version of your script, which is then sent out to production companies, agents, and possibly other contents where you can win funding for your movie. The logline helps you sell the idea of your movie overall which is why it is crucial to create a compelling, catchy, unique, and unforgettable one. A logline can make or break your success in Hollywood, before you even start. Make sure that you don't treat it as just an afterthought.

There are many factors that make up a good logline. At its core, it should be able to present the basic narrative without going into complex details of each character or the story. It should be as long as one sentence, at the most; while presenting the idea of:

1. **The main character.** Who the story is about?
2. **The goal.** What the main character is striving for?
3. **The opponent.** Who is standing in the way of the main character?

The Main character

When creating the logline and mentioning the main character, don't use the character name, as this may cause the reader confusion when reading your logline. The exception to this rule is if the story is about an important historical character or public figure. Now, instead of using a name, refer to a relatable occupation or status of the main character; such as businessman or American president. One of the biggest mistakes that amateur screenwriters make is that they use their characters to be their own voice of reason. Even if you are writing a story that's inspired by your own life or hardships, it's important to give your hero or main character their own existence. They shouldn't do or feel things just because it's how you're feeling, or how you would react to a certain situation. Remember that even famous people's biographies have to be rewritten to give them a dramatic edge; when it comes to creating personal stories some aspects should be embellished even just a little bit so that your story works.

When working with your main character, you can also attach a carefully chosen adjective to the main character as well, which is crucial in defining the character to your audience. For example:

"Brave soldier"
"Career----minded executive"

The Goal

The core of the screenplay is the main character's goal, which should be clearly presented in the logline. The entire drama of the story is hooked on the goal/s, and the obstacles faced by the main character as they attempt to achieve it. The first major goal should be presented at the first act of the screenplay, whether it is a psychological or physical goal.

The Opponent

The opponent forces represent the elements of the story which prevent the main character from reaching his goal. When writing about the opponent, be careful not to present too many details about the opponent but giving the reader the idea that loss or death is certainly the risk.

While you're at it, it's best that you also understand the most common mistakes writers make when creating their logline. Avoid these at all cost!

- **Too complex.** Even with a movie as complex, and with many layers such as Inception, you must be able to capture it. The logline must be able to simply and clearly express the entire idea of which the entire foundation of your story is built on.

- **No external quest.** Audiences want to be able to see the transformation from the inner quest to the external. But remember that most inner journeys have the same essence: all heroes want to achieve some sort of fulfillment or achievement. You've probably noticed by now that almost every movie has a theme where the hero transforms from child to adult; a coming of age sort of concept. This is what audiences want to hear about, how they did it, and how they succeeded.

- **Insufficient conflict.** Many writers don't understand that the lack of conflict is crucial to making the whole movie attractive in the first place. We all know through our own personal experiences that life can be tough and challenging, but why would you shell out your money to see a character rise to fame and succeed by doing less than what you do in your own daily life? We need to understand that the hero is going to do something challenging enough in order to achieve their goal. Ask yourself these questions: Does the quest sound difficult enough? Do you think that the goal seems impossible to achieve? Is the antagonism intimidating? If the answer to your questions are no, you can amplify the conflict factor by increasing the power of the opponent, or reducing the power of the main character.

- **Lacks originality.** Audiences want to see something that they haven't seen before. Work with novel ideas; something that people aren't expecting even with cliché characters. You should be familiar with many movies to be able to tell at this point if your logline is like something that's already been made. Better to ask for external validation; pitch your logline to your colleagues and friends and ask them if it reminds them of anything familiar. And if it does, adjust the elements of your story to make it unique.

It can be challenging, especially for first time scriptwriters, to create a compelling logline that will help you sell your script to producers and agents. Writing a short and sweet logline which is also exciting isn't easy. But it takes a lot of practice, so invest in some time for you to be able to write an effective logline. One of the most important advice I can give you about creating a logline, is to expose yourself to as many loglines as you can. Indulge in books, movies, and classic films, even movie reviews.
Understanding what went on the creative process of those writers creating meaningful loglines should help you in your own process, and eventually you'll get it nailed down. In the initial stages of writing your logline, you might even find that it starts out as longer than one sentence and being complicated. I suggest that you leave it as is for a few days, and think it over. Go back to it, and scratch out all the words that you feel do not contribute to the overall feel or heart of the story. You will eventually pare it down to its most basic core, and find yourself with a sentence that encapsulates the story's essence.

3. The 3 Act Structure

The three act structure is the glue that holds your screenplay together. The three parts are divided into: setup, confrontation, and resolution the primary building blocks to your story. All good stories follow the three act structure, it is fundamental to creating an effective script. Both your story and the scenes should follow it.

The three act structure is a widely used model that can be found in plays, novels, poetry, movies, and even video games. It was first conceptualized by Aristotle for his Poetics. This type of structure is evident even in the works of historical greats including Shakespeare, Hitchcock, and Aristotle. It's a foolproof method, tried and true structure for composing your movie and putting it together. It is a highly successful method, so I don't advise deviating from this structure which can cause great disappointment for potential producers, as well as your audience.

Act 1 – Setup

The setup makes up the first quarter of the story, and is where the main characters are introduced to the audience, called the exposition. It is used to reveal to the audience what the whole story is about. The setup also reveals the dramatic situation, or the context of your story. This part of your story should answer the questions who, what, when, and where, but it shouldn't yet reveal the why. It should also clearly communicate to the audience what the problems of the main character are, and establish their goals. Make your audience care about him or her. You know you've done a successful job at writing Act 1, when the viewer develops empathy for the main character.

The setup also features an inciting incident, which is an event that sets the entire plot of your story in motion. The general rule of thumb to pique and keep the interest of your audience is to reveal the main character and the supporting characters within the first ten minutes of the movie. If you make them wait any longer, they could get bored or forget about them.

Act 2 – Confrontation

The confrontation is the longest part of your script, which lasts approximately sixty minutes. If Act 1 reveals your character's goals, Act 2 should have your character chasing their goal. During Act 2, the main characters also meet their love interests if any, as well as any mentors who may support them throughout the rest of the film. This is also when the main character will face the obstacles or environments which will pose as a challenge to him, and as the confrontation evolves, the more danger or risk is exposed to the main character. In short, eventually the conflict between main character and opponent will be clearly felt.

The confrontation also features the first culmination, wherein the main character seems that they may be close to achieving their goal but by midpoint, they realize that they need to do more or everything else will fall apart. The midpoint is the scene which reflects a time in the main character's life where they feel that they are at their lowest, and therefore at the furthest possible stage from accomplishing their objective. Many times, this scene will cause the audience to think that the main character will eventually give up. The challenges that your main character will face during Act 2 helps bring your story to life, and as a result the viewer will become more involved with the story as a whole.

Most writers find that Act 2 is the most difficult to plot, and this is where they make the mistake of giving up. Do not! If you are starting out, remember that it's normal to feel stuck in this area for some time, but it will just give you a chance to think through the story even more thoroughly. But a trick that some of the brightest minds in Hollywood have discovered when they get stuck here is to go inside the mind of the opponent. All this time, you may have been spending too much time inside the main character's head, and it's your chance to switch sides for a bit. Working with a character that thinks the complete opposite way as your main character will give you a breath of fresh air, and the new perspective that you need to keep going with your story.

Act 3 – Resolution

The resolution is where the story culminates, sometimes with a renewed struggle in part of the main character. When you work on concluding your story, remember that you want the ending to be exciting yet unpredictable, while fulfilling your promise to the viewer. Ideally, the main character will achieve a goal that satisfies him, even though it's not always the goal that he had hoped for yet the viewer will accept as a good conclusion to the story.

The resolution contains a climax, where the battle is at its most intense both physically and emotionally, drawing the audience to grip their seats in suspense. Usually, the main character will fail, but you can creatively make them fail and try again until they end up succeeding, but in the process cause the audience to think that success for the main character may be impossible.

Following the climax is the denouement, the part where calm is restored back to the way things were in the beginning. But by this time, the characters have already changed as a result of the experiences and challenges they've had to go through, and are prone to facing difficulty adjusting to the equilibrium.

Because there is no clear cut formula on how scripts should end, it has become a very personal thing with writers in Hollywood. Scripts can even end up with a twist, and the final pages draw up an even more intense drama. But to have a good ending, be sure that you answer these questions:

1. Was the inciting incident or initial conflict resolved?
2. Was there another character conflict, which was also resolved?
3. How did you change the main character from the beginning to the end of the film?

The importance of the three act structure is that it helps writers create a dramatic flow of movement. In other words, it helps you make sure that things are consistently happening. Movement and change are significant in a well written screenplay, novel, book, or film. Then you work with this basic premise: hero plus obstacle equals conflict.

And what creates movement? Conflict, one conflict after another. Just make sure that you keep the focus on the main character or your main hero, and ensure that he continually explores dangerous or new territory so as to expose him to proper obstacles. Creating a story without the three act structure, one could say, is like building a house without a foundation. This will cause your walls to sag, the roof to collapse, and eventually the entire structure will self-destruct.

The last thing you want your audience to say about your movie is that it's predictable and boring. That's the biggest curse of all bad movies. The use of the three act structure avoids boredom to set in because it helps the writer think of things and events that cause conflict and change, which causes new conflict, and so on and so forth until the resolution is reached.

4. The Main Character

The main character of your story should be remembered, loved, and appreciated by your audience. The main character is responsible for telling your story and walks your audience through the same emotions as the character feels.

Good character development is crucial to every story; they shouldn't be stereotypical and should be more dimensional as the story evolves and as they interact with other characters. They should be responsive to transformation and emotion, and should be able to present their ideals, cultures, and beliefs throughout the story.

Creating a good main character requires deep thinking and research, as your goal is to create an entirely new person. Think about their history, background, biography, psychology, personality, and life goals. The audience needs to understand the main character's fears and goals as well. Use all your senses to breathe life into the main character as well other characters in the script. Cover their ancestry, occupations, physical characteristics and their unique traits. It is important that you're able to fully recognize them as if you know this person, and that you get under their skin. You should be able to conceptualize them and know them, inside out.

Effective character creation is one of the most exciting, yet challenging aspects of scriptwriting. It's difficult not to put your heart into it, because you need to realize a character who feels things, and not just a single dimensional dummy with cliché characteristics. They are not a puppet, they are the life of your story; they should be able to come alive.

The screenwriting process requires you, the writer, to answer the question: WHY? What is the character's role to play in the story? What is it that you yourself are feeling towards the character? Why does your character want what he wants?

And what is the passion of your character? It is also important that you know your character's vulnerable spot: what is their weakness? What is their kryptonite that causes their downfall? Once you start to piece together this information, you've got a story going. You'll understand more about the paths your character can take to achieve their goal without falling into their weakness, or what they need to do to overcome their fall. When you put your character into their predicament, you are successfully creating the dramatic core of your story.

The evolution of a character as the story progresses is referred to as the character arc. It is important because when we see a character change, we live vicariously through them, and essentially we are transformed along with them. Don't you notice that when you watch a great movie, you find yourself attached to the main character at some point; rooting for them until the movie ends with the character victorious? That's because good movies are made of characters that are so well written, that the audience can't help but get attached and involved with them.

Let's take for example the movie Miss Congeniality. FBI Agent Gracie Hart, played by
Sandra Bullock, had the goal of finding a terrorist who was targeting the Miss United States event. To achieve her goal, she had to go undercover as one of the contestants, but Gracie is as tomboy as tomboy comes, and the FBI team had to make her rediscover her feminine side again. All her life she's been used to being one of the boys, but now she had to be more feminine, soft, and weak, which to her doesn't make for a successful FBI agent. But it took a lot of effort for her to play the part of Ms. United States, and by the end of the movie she embraced her feminine side. Gracie allowed it to empower her and she was able to meet her goal, while changing from beginning to the end of the movie.

It should also be noted that even if your hero can be good in most situations, it's also important to give him some weaknesses. If he is clean and pure and has no bad side at all, he becomes very one dimensional, boring, and irrelevant to the audience. I will say this again and again throughout the book: audiences want something they can relate to, and as we all have major flaws, you wouldn't like someone that came without it, right? You want your audience to be able to root for him, and make him succeed and achieve his goals as a character. Your audience should have some fear that he may not make it. But if he is a perfect person, there will be no fear.

If there's one thing the audience love as well, it's a brave main character. Sometimes it isn't even what they are trying to accomplish that makes us love them, it's the lengths he's willing to go to accomplish it. He does brave things under pressure and dire circumstances, that we wish we could do.

Remember the movie, The Pursuit of Happiness, starring Will Smith? While everything seemed all right in the beginning of the movie, he eventually loses everything and is forced to think of creative ways to improve the quality of life for his son and himself. He takes steps moving forward to become successful, and succeeds when he becomes a millionaire.

Change shouldn't happen suddenly. It should be obvious from the beginning that the character can change, otherwise it will seem forced and not likely. Working with the character arc helps if you start with the beginning, the middle, and the end, to ensure gradual change.

Depending on the kind of story you're working on, your opponent can have a character arc as well. Remember that the character arc doesn't always have to be something positive, because drama from the movie can succeed with a main character who makes a change for the worse.

Suggested pointers to keep in mind when creating that memorable main character:

1. Gift your character with a sense of humor. People go to the movies for many reasons, and apart from entertainment we want to escape reality even for just two hours. The best way to escape reality is laughter, so make your character fun.
2. Create a talented character; give him talents that no one else has.
3. Give them a passion, which motivates them throughout the entire movie.
4. Last but not the least; we can't give any more emphasis on the importance of his willingness to change.

Now that you've got a main character, they are going to need someone whose main goal is to prevent the main character from succeeding: the opponent.

5. The Opponent

Great stories have a hero and they also have a villain. From comics to historical stories , villains have always played an important role in giving your story a powerful edge. They are responsible for mixing conflict into the story, acting as an obstacle to your main character all
throughout.

Having a good opponent is just as crucial to a good story, as the main character; therefore you should put just as much thought into the opponent as you would your hero. Having a person with the opposite goals as your main character gives the story an edge and a balance. If you put careful thought into your main character but not your opponent, your script will lack balance causing the conflict to be weak and lose its appeal.

Your story can have one or more opponents, but it is essential to carefully create their role to help create the narrative tension you are looking for. A good opponent will have the audience on their seat, wanting to know more about how the story will unfold. The audience will want the main character to be able to beat him. Good storytelling, ideally, should gift the opponent with even just a few saving graces. Sometimes, opponents start off on the side of the main character, but due to certain circumstances, become the character's opponent.

Think about the strengths the opponent should have. He should have specific characteristics that give him power over the hero, but he should also have his own weaknesses. He must also be able to protect himself from the main character's strengths. In order to preserve the balance of the story, give both the hero and the opponent the same amount of strengths and weaknesses. The real conflict arises then, when are you are able to make one capitalize on the weakness of the other, with the hero coming out as successful in the end.

At its core, the opponent evokes feelings of hatred from the audience. But there are also some villains who are so good at what they do, they become unforgettable and because the audience hates him so much, he becomes powerful. This is why many of us even have our favorite villains. Suggested pointers for you to consider when creating your opponent:

- The opponent doesn't always have to be a villain, or human for that matter
- He should be at least as smart or more powerful than the main character
- Has its own character arc, or sort of personal transformation. In fact, the opponent could even be considering changing into a better person as the main character gains power over him, or he becomes more desperate. Either way, the battle should also change him at the end of the story.
- Should be feared enough by the main character so much that the audience remains hooked to their seat in fear of the main character's failure
- Constantly tosses challenges to the main character's way, constantly keeping him on his feet and thinking of new ways to defy the opponent. The opponent can fall into several categories:

Immoral Opponent

This is one of the most popular types of opponents you can choose from. Their distinction from the hero is as clear as day and night, black and white. This makes it easy for viewers to take sides. It can come in the form of a hypocrite, who exudes goodness, sweetness, and kindness on the surface but comes with bad intentions. And because the hypocrite is able to fool the good guy, the viewers hate him even more.

The immoral opponent can also take the shape of the psycho, who is made up of pure unadulterated evil. The psycho is present in psychological dramas and thrillers, as well as horror stories. They're the serial killers, mass murderers... you get the picture. And they drive fear to the heart of the audience, because they themselves are terrified of them, whether he's a fictional or non-fictional character.

The immoral opponent can also be presented as a normal person who succumbed to their weakness, whether it is greed, lust, and extreme hatred. These emotions could drive them to a dangerous point where they put the main character's safety at risk, and there's your conflict.

Moral Opponent

The moral opponent presents a more complex character, because he comes with more layers for the audience to peel off and understand. They often do what they think is the right thing, but the conflict of your story requires him to come into battle with your main character.

He could be a good guy on a different team; and while he means no harm on your hero, they stand on two separate grounds that rev the engine of conflict and evoke negative emotions. Examples of this are lawyers who stand for different causes, or a love triangle where two men are fighting over the same woman. These types of stories can open doors for different types of outcomes relating to morality and life's big questions.

The moral opponent can also come in the form of a crusader, who's downright scary. He is motivated by the passion of his cause, and when faced with a dilemma he works with what he believes is the lesser evil. He may also be someone who is fanatic about his passion, which can cause him to make dangerous decisions, putting the main character at risk.

Lastly, he could also come in the form of a normal good person, who out of desperation resorts to illegitimate means as they feel that there is no other choice.
The immoral and moral opponent explains that not all opponents have to be evil. They can have many complexities, which is why you'll notice that in some movies the opponents aren't exactly evil. Opponents can be further broken down into two categories:

- **The Scene Opponent**

The scene opponent's main job is to provide an obstacle to keep the main character from achieving their goal in every scene. Everything that the scene opponent wants, is the complete opposite of the main character. And whenever the scene opponent appears, he provides tension, causing jeopardy, and resulting in keeping the audience tense. If you are going to make use of the scene opponent, make sure that when you are going over each scene, it is clear what the goal is. Be careful not to overdo it, as then you will just cause one bad situation to happen after the other, which makes for a bad action movie.

- **The Big Troublemaker**

Big troublemakers have the capacity to make things change, and give the main character a run for his life. His impact on the main character is so massive that it makes the viewer think the main character stands no chance in the way of the big troublemaker. While the character of the troublemaker doesn't necessarily have to be terrifying, he possesses a power that no other character in the movie has. This makes for excellent conflict, which is what viewers love.

I should also stress here, that the big troublemaker doesn't have to be human. It exemplifies the weakness of the main character, and it could be something that poses extreme difficulty in overcoming. It could be an addiction to alcoholism, such as in the
movie 28 Days. It could also be a powerful natural disaster, such as a storm. It could
even be in the form of an ideology.

6. The Supporting Cast

Now you know what it takes to make a good screenplay but your ultimate goal is to produce a great screenplay. One wherein people can relate to, and discuss the dynamics of the relationships that the characters had within the movie. This is where
the role of supporting characters come in; they should be as complex as the main character, but it is also your job to ensure that the main character and his relationship with the supporting cast is crucial to the story you are trying to tell.

Writers, when starting out, tend to take the value of supporting characters for granted. Most screen writing seminars emphasize the importance of the main character. But let's face it: the relationships we have define us as humans, and certainly make our life more interesting, not to mention the fact that it provides many dimensions and contrasts to our lives. Especially our close friends and confidantes. Can you imagine life without your close friends? Can you imagine telling the story of your life without the presence of your own supporting cast? In the same way, don't tell your main character's story without their own confidant. The presence of a "close friend" will enhance the audience's view of the main character, and help them relate to them on higher levels.

Take into consideration the following close friends, who have made an impact to the audience:

1. **My Best Friend's Wedding.** What would Julianne do without her gay best friend, George, whom she would confide in and talk to whenever she was sad? George played a vital role as he helped lift her spirits, and make Julianne's character happy, and even laugh, during the times she felt she didn't meet her

character's goal: which was to marry her best friend, Michael.

2. **Lethal Weapon.** What would Roger do without his funny buddy, Roger? The famous duo have been applauded for entertaining audiences together so much that it's almost difficult to imagine one without the other.

3. **Pretty in Pink.** Duckie plays one of Andie's best friends, who acts like a goofball in the movie to disguise his true feelings for her. One can't help but feel bad for his character, and he stops talking to Andie when he finds out she is going to marry Blaine.

4. **Romy and Michelle's High School Reunion.** Romy and Michelle play one of the movie world's favorite best friend duos. They confided in each other and even argued a few times, but towards the end they made for such an entertaining duo who helped each other achieve their character's goals.

One of the most effective methods you can create a great supporting character through the close friend is to create contrasts between their personalities. The role of a close friend for the main character is to provide emotional support and have faith in the main character, give them tools to succeed, motivate them, and even increase their personal stakes in the story. During the main character's struggles, and during the moments they are low or encounter flounders, audiences love to watch how the best friend or sidekick pushes them on, because that's what they are designed to do.

Here are some forms of the most famous supporting character types you may want to inject into your script:

1. **The party girl.** She gets to act out the main character's main passions, especially if the main character plays a shy, introverted role. Sometimes, she even says things that the main character wishes she could say, helping string together essential parts of the movie. The party girl could be in the form of a person who even eggs on the main character to get into trouble. Remember the Wedding Crashers? Jeremy and John play two best friends who crash parties together, and get into tons of trouble together. In the Black Swan, the role was portrayed well by Mila Kunis, who helped Natalie Portman's character confront her deep, dark fears.

2. **Mother figure.** The mother figure or mentor plays the role of being a wise, charming counsel to the main character. She provides practical advise on how the main character should move about her goals, and sometimes even die with the goal of moving the story forward. A great example would be Aunt May from The Amazing Spiderman.

3. **The doormat.** This is one type of supporting character who is usually the brains behind the story's operations. They help create plans and do the necessary expositional work for the main character, and sometimes have passive characters, which cause the main character to take them for granted sometimes. The doormat is the rational close friend, who tries to do things to help make the main character evolve, and grow up. Ron Weasley in the Harry Potter series is a great example of the doormat.

4. **Father figure.** If your main character is flawed because they had a real father who may have died when they were young, ignored him, or left him, the father figure plays an important supporting role because he fills that gap. Because of him, the main

character can move on and accomplish his goals. An example of the helpful father figure is the role of Alfred, in the Batman movies.

Because your main character will have their own flaws, the best friend is an important aspect that provides depth and character to your story. They take the form of real persons we'd be able to encounter in real life, even if it's just the bartender that your main character visits every time he feels that he is hindered from his goal. Be creative but seek purpose when creating the best friend or confidant character.

Creating a character can be challenging enough, especially when you're just starting out. Now imagine that you have to create many of them. The trick here is to prevent your supporting characters from seeming like cookie cut outs. They should be as interesting as your main characters. Read on for suggested pointers on creating unforgettable supporting characters:

- **Give them the illusion of an arc.** Unlike major characters whose character arcs have to be much more carefully planned, with supporting characters it can just change over the course of the movie without much explanation. By page 100 your character can hate children, yet a couple hundred pages later all of a sudden he likes them. And this is totally fine.

- **Introduce your characters in two important sequences in the movie.** The first should be in the background, while the second time should be in the foreground. During the first time your audience meets the main character's best friend, it could be in passing, but later on you can introduce more detail that will give the audience more information as to why their role is crucial to helping the main character achieve their main goal. During the second introduction, your audience may not recognize them right away but they'll have that light bulb moment that helps them recognize who this character is, and later on help them piece the story together. Doing this creates a sense of familiarity; where the audience just experienced a character in passing before but now is more relevant to the plot of the story.

- **Associate them with a particular place,** so that whenever the audience comes across that certain location, they already become familiar with the close friend or supporting character. This place could be anywhere; a favorite café, a beach, or a bar. Giving them a place of their own makes the supporting character more life like.

- **Work on creating character flaws for them as much as you would the main character and the opponent.** Nothing is more forgettable in a movie than a character that has no flaws, or seeks to be pure and full of virtue. That gets boring fast. In the same way, having a character with no flaws makes it seem like you're just trying to get them to be the writer's mouthpiece and insert yourself into the dialogue of the movie. Do something that the audience will remember, such as giving them a unique way of talking or giving them an identifiable flaw such as destructive or bad habits.

- **Your main character should have at least one defining characteristic.** Just like the best friends of our own real lives, everyone close to us has a unique trait that
we associate lovingly with them.

7. Love Interest

The love interest doesn't have to be a real person, but it is what the main character is willing to fight for, or is portrayed as his or her ultimate passion in the movie. The love interest is the main character's goal, what they hope to achieve at the end of the movie, and this should be as clear as day and night.

One of the biggest mistakes writers make in the beginning is by giving the main character a really vague goal. I've actually read some screenplays where the main character does nothing but jump from one situation to another, then before you know it, it's the end of the story. They didn't really accomplish anything significant. If these types of stories made it to the big screen, the audience would have no idea what the story is really all about, because the main character didn't' make any actual changes in his or her life. And yes, your audience will zone out from boredom.

Think about it this way: if someone asks you what the main character's goal is, avoid vague answers such as "to get together with the girl of his dreams", or "to be happier", or "to meet financial independence". Because these answers are so vague, it can be difficult to know if he was really able to accomplish them. What you want is a tangible goal for the main character, because you want the audience to root for him and see it to fruition no matter what it will take in the story. What does it mean for your character to be happy? What will it take for him to be in a relationship with the girl of his dreams? What will he need to do in order to become rich and successful? These are the things that you need to consider.

The love interest, or the main character's want, is what drives the entire story. Although characters may have different wants in each scene, they ultimately still have one major goal which is different from what they want.

Sometimes, the character is even unaware of this need. This is why it's important to establish what they want, versus what they need. Let's break this down further.

As you work through the attainment of achieving the main character's goal, the want is something that they are conscious of. This want is usually revealed within the first act, where the main character will be able to express that they "want to win that game", or "want to win that girl", or "catch the bad guy". However, the main character's goal can shift as a secondary goal eventually emerges. This goal is not new, but rather a need that comes to the surface.

The want is something external, while the need is something internal. Remember that. In a nutshell, the main character's need is something that defines the character's overall essence; what he's made of, or a part of them that has been suppressed for quite some time. It works together with the main character's want when it comes to structuring their goal. This is evident in many movies, where for example on the outside the character is a workaholic whose character changes when a situation taps into their core, which reveals their loving or more human character.

Similarly, even the opponent will have their own goals from the very beginning. Maybe one of them just wants to be able to work in peace, or be able to get some sleep. It can be as simple as that. But events throughout the movie can turn their worlds upside down, leading them to clash head on as they each try to accomplish their own wants and needs. Both the lives of the main character and opponent are then pulled out of their lives and set out on a quest that they both didn't imagine they would have to at the beginning.

Examples of wants versus needs:

- Man wants to grieve for the murder of his father, but realizes that he must set out to find justice by looking

for the convicted murderer to save him from harming his brother.
- Woman wants to look for her real father, but needs to leave her hometown after 25 years of living there.
- An ex-cop wants to track down a serial killer who's out to plant a bomb, but he has only 5 days and needs to work hard for the investigation.

Throughout the process of writing your script, you will constantly have to ask yourself what it is your character wants. Their actions will be based by this motivation, their love interest, and their goal, combined with their overall personality traits that you've
assigned to them as you drew their character.

8. Accelerating Moment

The "Something Big Happens" also known as the hook, is the epicenter of your script. Its what you will be using to pitch your screenplay, and prove to producers that your story is a profitable one.

Ideally, the hook should be established within the first five pages of your screenplay. Ever since the MTV generation, people have had much shorter attention spans, and for the screenwriter this means that you must get the audience more interested in a shorter span of time. This means you need to get the movie going. Suspense, horror, and crime stories have used murder or death as their version of something big happens, but because it's been used so many times already it's practically cliché. Therefore if you decide to use this, make sure that the rest of the journey is an interesting one. Other popular types of big events could be a meteor landing on earth – that sort of thing. You get it.

Now you can learn about not just successfully writing a hook, but how to make a powerful one. I'd say that a powerful hook causes the audience to raise questions. Make sure that the question is relevant and related to the rest of the story.

Let's look at a famous example: In the movie Silence of the Lambs, where the new FBI girl, Clarice, is tossed into the underground world of psychopathic killers. It is an excellent example of a hook because it leads you to ask if Clarice will successfully retrieve information while making it out alive. In the 1995 movie Swingers, about a group of friends who live in Hollywood and confront dating problems, there is a subtle hook in the form of making the audience question of Mike will end up breaking down, and calling the girl he's been obsessing with. The question works with the rest of the journey, as Mike's character evolves, therefore integrating it seamlessly with the rest of the script. You can even be as bold as you like; think of Betty Blue: the movie pretty much starts with the lead characters naked, descending into their beach house and caught within the passionate moments of lovemaking. That's the kind of thing that really hooks the audience to your story. Go back to all your favorite movies in all genres, and ask yourself, at which scene did the movie really reel you in? Examine how the films started. Because you as the screenwriter have the power to create the same effect in your very first screenplay. By writing, you can set the mood, create the necessary tones, and toss your audience into the story by setting off a big event that they won't be able to get out of their heads until the movie helps them answer a question. It's an important event and scene that guides them in through the rest of your story; it creates a purpose for the climax and the ending. Upon experiencing the hook, the audience knows that by the end of the movie, the question will be resolved by the antagonist, protagonist, or even the theme and central question.

Amateur writers tend to make the mistake of wasting their first few pages by filling it up with dull dialogue; don't make the same mistake. The first few pages are just as important, if not more, because this is the reason why people will stay to watch your movie instead of walking out from boredom.

9. Emotional Decision

The main character has to respond to the big event; this means he or she needs to do something which they are not excited about. The call to action also referred to as the inciting incident, is basically an event that significantly changes the characters life.

Take for example the movie Armageddon, which involves many exciting scenes. At the onset, you may think that the call to action was when the first meteor had obliterated the Space Shuttle, eventually striking the earth. Or, it could also be the scene when Truman discovered the serious, fatal consequences of the asteroid the size of Texas which is flying towards earth. None of the above! The real call to action here is when Harry Stamper, played by Bruce Willis, was summoned to work for NASA. This was a decision he had to make, to meet his needs, even though he and his loved ones were afraid.

The call to action can also be referred to as the call to adventure, precisely because as I mentioned it's a situation that pulls the character out of his comfort zone. It will help the viewer learn clearly about the main character's goals. The call to action doesn't necessarily have to be a huge, profound event. It can be as simple as a phone call, although this part of your script plays a very important role for the rest of the movie. It sets the wheels moving in the audience's mind of what the climax could be like.

You can't create a compelling story without the call to action. If you did, what this would result is a whole bunch of characters running around with no real goal in sight. Now you may be wondering, when exactly does the call to action happen?

For some stories and genres, the call to action can even happen right before the movie starts, although that is very rare. For the most part, it happens within the first 28 pages of your script, but to the audience, this occurs after you've already introduced the hero, and shown the audience what his life is really like. But it can also happen after the exposition. In the movie Rocky, the inciting incident came very late. The main character will react to the call of action, and in fact he may even be able to resist it, until Act One breaks. This is followed by hooking your audience in, and the hero will commit to the adventure. The adventure could be something physical, psychological, emotional, or even a combination of all these.

Something you must remember when creating your main character's call to action: this is not an active moment, but rather something that happens to your character. It is not something that he actively pursues or engages in. The first act would usually have the hero dealing with the consequences of the inciting incident, but then eventually he would need to decide if he is going to get in deeper or not.

The inciting incident takes the film from an orderly structure to one of chaos. Look at it as the point of no return. After the inciting incident, there is no way that things could get back to normal unless the main character accomplishes his goal. Now it's time for you to confront some questions: What is it that your characters want? What is preventing them from getting it?

If your main character succeeds, it will be a happy ending. But if he doesn't, it's a tragedy or a drama. The inciting incident will make your audience stop and think about this question. This spurs the actions in place, it starts the guesswork to see if the person they're rooting for will win or not.

Examples of inciting incidents:

- **Legally Blonde.** When Warner broke up with Elle, while she was expecting him to propose to her.
- **Gladiator.** When Marcus Aurelius, the emperor, requested for Maximus to be Rome's steward.
- **Chronicles of Narnia.** Lucy's discovery that the wardrobe is her key that leads her to Narnia.
- **Clockwork Orange.** When Georgie proposes that the gang should pull a real heist, as he asserts himself to Alex
- **Star Wars.** When Luke Skywalker sees the holographic image of Princess Leia, asking for help
- **Alien.** When the crew successfully lands on the planet, but finds a deserted, wrecked alien spaceship
- **Jerry Maguire.** When Jerry puts the Mission Statement on the mailbox of everyone in the office, yet he has second thoughts What makes a great inciting incident makes the audience have a flashback of everything else that came before it in the movie, and realize that everything they thought would happen or was true is actually false. Again, the key here is to keep the audience in suspense, and avoid predictability at all cost.

Suggested pointers to remember when writing the inciting incident:

1. Don't make the audience wait too long.

Rocky was a famous movie with a late inciting incident but it succeeded because this was written by professional scriptwriters. You want to take gradual steps to learn about how to pace your characters and the events in the movie. Follow the basic formula of writing inciting incidents early on in the film, because this is what will keep your audience engaged in the movie.

2. This is the event that will drive the rest of the story, so make sure it's attention catching and interesting.

The viewers should want to know what's going to happen after the main character responds or refuses the call to action. Is the detective going to meet the same fate as the other victims? Is he going to find the killer? You want the audience glued to their seats.

3. Last but not the least, make sure that it's believable.

Don't do things that will have your audience saying: " Why on earth did they do that??" If the call to action isn't believable, you will lose audience engagement right away.

10. Main Character's Goal

Now is the time to really think about the goal of your character, you need to confront the type of change you want to see happen to your character. What kind of improvement over their current situation do you want to happen? What kind of improvement do they need to meet their goal? What is it that they need to do to return to a situation when things were better than they are right now?

The goal is very important for the main character, this is the reason why they hold on to it very tightly despite the various obstacles and emotional setbacks they may be encountering throughout the movie.

Main characters in well developed stories can even have two main goals. There is the story goal, which involves all the other characters in the movie. This goal affects the other characters as well. Then there is the inner conflict or the personal goal. Remember that the reason that they are the main character is because they make choices that help them resolve their inner conflict and this choice also has a role to play in determining how the overall story goal will be resolved.

Some examples from famous movies:

- In Star Wars, when Luke Skywalker decides to go with his gut feel instead of his computer, which helps him kill the Death Star.
- When Romeo and Juliet decide to commit suicide rather than to face a life without each other, this leads to an understanding between their two families.

There are also some stories when the main character can lack an inner conflict, but you'll notice that these stories tend to lack emotional substance. On the other hand, stories which don't have an overall goal can create a picture of a main character who is then too emotional but doesn't really give any shape to the goal of the film. This leads to a movie that seems plotless, and eventually, pointless.

If you are working on a longer film, you can give your main character additional goals, also known as subplots. But when writing these subplots, make sure that you carefully consider them so that they have a meaningful contribution to the entire theme of the story.

Since we're on the topic as well, I should add that not only should the main character or the main character have a goal, but the opponent should have one too. The goals of the opponent should be in conflict with those of the main character.

Here are the reasons why main character goals are crucial to your story:

1. Goals tighten the plot line.

You've probably come across scripts before, or movies, where you simply end up asking yourself, "Where are they going with this?" A plot that seems lost, or without a point, is one without clear cut character goals. If your audience ask themselves this question, this means that the plotline is weak, and you haven't done your job as a writer. The only time that the audience should rightfully ask this question, is if it was your point in the first place to misguide them so as to catch them by surprise.

You need to create strong goals for your main characters because this will avoid you having scenes that slow down the entire plot. A tight plot will prevent your audience from taking a break, because by then your audience will care too much to leave the story alone.

2. Good character goals make your story believable.

When you're starting out, it's completely normal to have several scenes that don't really have any goals. But as you're going over your first drafts, it is crucial that you address these issues. For example, if your character continually keeps running into dilemmas without it getting sorted out, the story will get ridiculous fast and the audience will get bored. This is because they have no clear goals to drive the story. After some time, these dilemmas will keep piling on top of each other and not sound logical.

3. Having character goals can help simplify your workload. This is true because if your character's goals are clear cut, it will be their main passion and will drive them consistently throughout the different scenes. The main character will keep thinking about their goal instead of idly engaging in conversation with other characters about pointless issues.

Instead of having to always think about how to insert your character in certain scenes, having that goal in mind will reduce your stress and time thinking about how to do that. Your character is simply pursuing their goals, and taking the steps that they need to take to accomplish what it is they are set out to do.

During the course of writing, try to set your main character's goals early on. Over time you may find that you may want to change the goal, and that's completely fine. As the character's goal changes, you'll also have to give allowance to change the outcome of your story.

Goals don't always have to be complicated. They can be grand, they can even be small, but what's important is that you keep enough of them to ensure there is tension in the story. The goal can be happy, sad, exciting, terrifying, or even scary, because the entire story is about how the character achieves the goal anyway.

When you give your character a goal, you are giving them a purpose. It's the sole reason that they are in the story in the first place. To achieve that goal, there will be obstacles to be overcome, creating the weave of tension in your story. There is no scientific formula that addresses any set rules about how characters achieve their goal, as this lies entirely in the hands of the writer. Be gentle with yourself, don't give yourself too hard a time when it comes to creating the obstacles. The audience will enjoy the conflict, and so should you.

One last piece of advice when creating the goal and conflict: just make sure your character isn't exactly sailing through life without difficulty. You want them to be relatable, and let's face it: real life is tough. Your character should face challenges in their journey, just like we do when we are trying to accomplish a difficult goal.

11. Genre

In its essence, the genre is defined based on the thematic narrative elements
based on which the structure of your story is created. It's important to understand what kind of genre you'll be using, because the key to creating a
compelling script and sellable story is to carefully manage your audience's expectations.

Most film genres are borrowed from the literary genres, which categorizes films in the following ways:

- The action genre is usually characterized by high energy chases, physical stunts, battle scenes, and non-stop motion. To sum it up, action films are basically where continuous physical action takes the priority over storytelling; or basically it does the job of storytelling. This type of stories usually has a hero that has such a great goal, with seemingly impossible odds to overcome it.

- Adventure films are exciting in the sense that they pique the audience's interest by placing the characters in exotic locations, or place them in exciting situations. In adventure films, the main character is placed in the center of a great conquest or exploration, usually where the main goal is to pursue something unknown to them. The plot is usually sprinkled with multiple suspense scenes and puzzles to be solved.

- Comedies are films whose main goals are to evoke laughter from the audience through light hearted plots and other methods which include use of language, action, sarcasm, and exaggerated situations within characters. There are many forms of comedic styles to choose from, including romantic comedies, slapstick, spoofs, parodies, and dark satirical comedies. Some comedy flicks make use of serious material, although more often than not the ending is usually a happy one.

- Crime and gangster movies revolve around the lives of mobsters or criminals. They could take the form of underworld leaders or robbers, basically people who operate outside the law as their own way of life. Crime movies usually highlight the life of a famous mobster or criminal, or tell the story of his rise and fall, power struggles with the law, or even rival gangs. These types of films are usually set in ultra crowded cities to give a contrast to the life of the criminal; one who lives his life in secret.

- Drama films are serious, emotional, and thought provoking films. The stories resemble real life issues and tense situations with life like characters, usually whom the audience can very much relate to. Unlike other genres, dramas don't make use of much special effects, action, or comedy to get the point across; the characters portrayed often have to work with a serious conflict either with themselves or external forces around them, human or not. Dramatic movies usually cover a wide spectrum of themes dealing with the human emotion; it could be racial prejudice, societal ills, drug addiction, religious intolerance, alcoholism, violence, mental illness, or similar topics.

- Epics or historical films usually deal with a historic or imagined event; where the plot contains figures of the mythical, legendary, or heroic kind. The characters are placed in exotic settings, wear lavish costumes especially in period films, and the background music all play a part in telling a story that happened in the past. The settings are large and elaborate, and make use of a large number of cast members to recreate that historic feeling in old towns and cities.

- Horror films have only one goal in mind: that is to drive as much terror and fear into the heart of the audience. These types of movies uncover our own dormant fears and awaken us in a most shocking way. Horror movies are dark, and tell stories through odd, strange events that could be fictional or non fiction. Horror films work well with science fiction when they make use of alien invasion or other ghastly monsters that don't exist; and make use of special effects to deal with supernatural matters such as those of the living dead, witches, and other gothic elements. Modern horror stories usually entail the use of Satanic and evil elements, unfriendly ghosts, poltergeists, and haunted houses.

- Musicals and dance films are cinematic types of films where characters tell the story in full scale dance and song routine. The film narrative usually already has musical scenes built into it, or certain scenes require the characters to burst out into song at unexpected moments. Traditional musicals are made up of specifically chosen cast members who do the signing as their way of telling the story. Of all the genres, musicals are also considered the most escapist genre, with the ultimate goal of the characters usually searching for a love, popularity and acceptance, or wealth.

- Science fiction films have the whole ensemble: special effects, heroes, villains, exotic locations, futuristic technology, unknown forces, and fanciful production design to make the settings and characters look seamlessly real. Science fiction films are usually set in a time or location other than the here and now, such as traveling to distant planets, time traveling, and elements of fantasy.

It's also important to learn about the various types of genres because you don't want to confuse people. If you're starting out in the industry, it's best to stick with a genre that you're familiar with, and one that you already like because you're already familiar with the type of writing that certain genre will entail.

The genre that you choose will reflect a certain perspective and attitude about the story you're trying to tell, although it doesn't necessarily reflect your own perspective. The genres discussed above are capable of telling a story in many different ways. For example, if you're trying to tell the story of a plane that's about to crash, you can put it in many different angles that it could even have a light hearted humorous way of telling it that it's good enough to be placed in the comedy genre. It could even be dramatic; a type of movie that makes people ponder life and death questions. As you can see here, the selection of genre is really about the emphasis of the theme that you wish to relay to the audience.

The challenge here is to make your story relatable enough, regardless of the genre you choose. All good stories tell us something about the human condition. In horror movies, we are forced to confront or biggest fears. In drama, we can examine different versions of ourselves or confront how certain situations would make us react. Now, you get the point, right?

12. Theme

Have you ever heard someone complain about seeing a movie and it feels like they've seen the movie before only with different characters and surroundings? This is because movies often revolve around a certain number of themes, but it's the way the story is told that makes it different. The great challenge here is how you, the storyteller, can take a concept that has been told many different ways and take the world by storm just by your interpretation of it.

The theme of your story is vital to the entire screenplay. The whole purpose should be to explore an underlying truth, or moral; or try to say something about what the screenwriter wants to say. Well conveyed themes are usually cultivated from writers who have experienced something first hand, because those types of movies have a passion that speaks through them. Ask yourself what you are passionate about, then use that to get your story going.

The theme or the moral of the story, is the clear point that you want your audience to realize once they have seen the movie. It forms the foundation for the rest of your story, which is why a clear understanding of it is crucial to the effectiveness of the overall storytelling. This can be one of the biggest mistakes of first time writers: not investing enough time to fully understand the theme that they want to portray. Once you've gotten a clearer grasp on your theme, write it down on a post it. In the beginning this may be difficult because you're trying to distill it to its most basic essence. Put the post it wherever you work to remind you of the core focus and theme of your entire screenplay.

Once you fully understand your theme, it's time to string together all the elements of your story so that it all reflects the same moral.

Here's a look at the central themes used in movies:

1. **Good versus Evil.** This is the major struggle that's found in many comic books, films, movies, and even in our own very culture. Good is characterized by cast members who exhibit honor, loyalty, and courage while bad is portrayed by characters who show they are selfish, capable of betrayal, and cowardice. Stories with this type of central theme usually show that good always prevails, but there are still some very well written movies where evil wins, such as in Star Wars Episode V. Good versus evil is a classic theme used in movies because it shows the ultimate showdown between characters who are extreme opposites.

2. **Love conquers all.**

Everyone loves a great love story, and Hollywood will never run short of them. It can fit in all kinds of genres, as we all consider love to be the most noble pursuit of man. Love is certainly the strongest force in the world, and the most powerful, compelling theme you can use to tell a story.

3. **Triumph over hardship.**

Almost all movies have a main character that needs to get out of a difficult situation. And when they are able to succeed, it's no surprise that the audience can walk out of the cinema feeling good about themselves because they were rooting for the character to win. Films that are centered around this theme have the hardship defining the main character's story, such as in the movie Slumdog Millionaire. It almost always revolves around a person with noble intentions and a good heart that was placed unfortunately in dire circumstances, yet they triumph over it. People love these kinds of movies because they tell the story of the unbeatable human spirit even in the face of challenging circumstances.

4. Man vs. Society.

When man goes against social norms or traditions, this often makes for a good story especially when you feature a main character who sacrifices his own dignity for the sole purpose of standing up for a cause. A good example is the story of Erin Brockovich, a woman who used all the resources she could get to defeat a power company who was causing people to become poisoned. The characters basically sacrifice whatever they can to meet their goals in the movie, whether it's to uphold societal acceptance or social injustices.

5. **Death as part of the cycle of life.** Death is one of the most confrontational and emotional topics you can have as a theme to your story. It can be the death of a family member, child, spouse, or even pet, and when the story is told well this will certainly hit a chord. Even in the movie Hachiko, about a dog whose owner passed away, the dog never stopped waiting for his owner's return in the same train station months after his death. It tells the story of loyalty and unconditional love that pets have for their owners, and you'd be hard pressed to find a dry eye after one sees the movie. Films can explore issues that deal with grief and loss, and embed this into the movie's narrative, while successfully telling a story.

6. Revenge.

One of the most popular themes is revenge, where the endings can vary. In certain movies, the opponents are justified such as in Mean Girls, or the person seeking revenge makes the outcome less desirable, such as in Carrie. No matter what the ending, revenge movies are always about the journey to obtaining justification for one's feelings whether you're the one being hurt or the one hurting others.

7. Coming of age.

This is a classic theme that centers around a young main character who is made to face the adult world and all its complexities and challenges. Sometimes they are thrown into it by accident where they aren't ready to face the consequences of their actions, such as in Juno. Other times the main character may be more than eager to step into the adult world, such as in Sixteen Candles. The coming of age theme could make use of a lighter plot, such as the character going through the social norms or trying to break out of introversion to be accepted, such as attending parties or drinking with peers. On the other hand, it could also make use of more serious issues such as how trauma, death, divorce, or even abuse can change the character and force them to maturity.

8. Man vs. Nature.

There has always been a fascination with how man can overcome the powerful forces that is Nature in itself, especially with those that threaten to completely annihilate mankind until the characters level up or find a promising solution. We love apocalypse themed movies, as well as those that show man literally struggling with forces of nature, such as in Jaws.

13. Conclusion

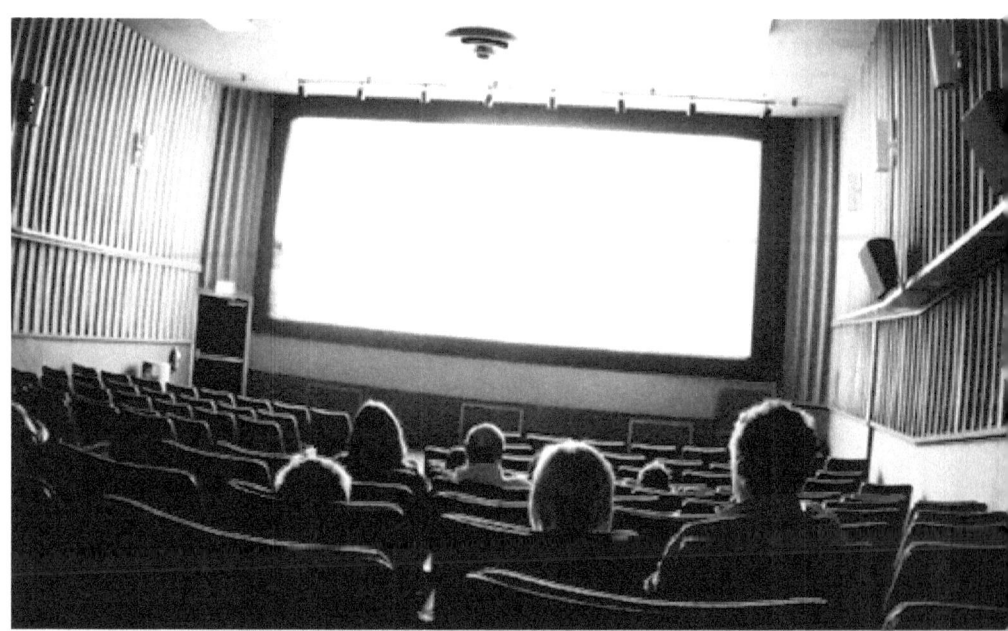

Creating a successful screenplay is not easy. It's a long term commitment and it will take time, dedication, and practice for one to effectively hone their skills at the craft. However, Hollywood's standards for successful movies won't change, and there are tools of the trade to help you do what you can do best. There are formulas and structures as we've discussed in this book to guide you.

Given all these tools to create your foundation, it is your job as the writer to bring an original voice and method of storytelling to Hollywood. People will never tire of seeing new material, or a traditional story told through a fresh perspective. Do what you need to do to keep your creative juices flowing; live a good healthy life, and keep yourself surrounded by things that constantly inspire you.

Over the years, you'll find that whether you're writing your first, second, or tenth screenplay, you'll always go back to the formulas we've discussed above. You've done a good job of taking advantage of arming yourself with industry knowledge and skills which you'll master eventually.

Think of these elements as a recipe, which you'll fine tune over time. It's a recipe that you're working to perfect, yet you'll find that various situations will call for you to spend longer in one area than the other. Maybe for some stories, character development will be a breeze; while for others, working on the main character's goal will be more challenging.

No matter what the obstacles are that gets in your way, or when you feel like quitting, don't succumb. Keep a notebook with you at all times, where you can jot down ideas, words, and thoughts that come to play. As a creative, we never really know when the best ideas are going to hit us. It could be during your morning coffee, while you're having brunch, listening to music, or even watching a movie. You could even draw inspiration from people you meet in your daily lives, and weave them into a new interesting character for your next screenplay. Screenwriting will be a lifelong process. Commit to a writing schedule and give yourself ample time and space daily to commit to the writing process. Evolution as a screenwriter is gradual, so don't be so hard on yourself if you aren't getting the immediate response that you've hoped for. Stick to your plans and your story, because you will get there.

Hollywood is a tough market, but you'll make it with the guidelines I've provided for you. These are foolproof methods on how to make it in the cutthroat industry. The adventure for you, the storyteller, has now officially begun. There's no way to go back up, and there's no better time to start honing your skills than right here and right now. Thanks for picking up this book; I look forward to seeing your screenplay on the movies one day!

14. THANK YOU FOR READING !

Thank You so much for reading this book. If this title gave you a ton of value, It would be amazing for you to leave a REVIEW !